Orphan Hours

ALSO BY STANLEY PLUMLY

POETRY

Old Heart

Now That My Father Lies Down Beside Me:
New and Selected Poems, 1970–2000

The Marriage in the Trees

Boy on the Step

Summer Celestial

Out-of-the-Body Travel

Giraffe

How the Plains Indians Got Horses

In the Outer Dark

NONFICTION

Posthumous Keats

Argument & Song: Sources & Silences in Poetry

Orphan Hours

POEMS

Stanley Plumly

W. W. NORTON & COMPANY · NEW YORK · LONDON

For information about permission to reproduce selections from this book,
write to Permissions, W. W. Norton & Company, Inc.,
500 Fifth Avenue, New York, NY 10110

For information about special discounts for bulk purchases, please contact
W. W. Norton Special Sales at specialsales@wwnorton.com or 800-233-4830

Manufacturing by Courier Westford
Book design by Brooke Koven
Production manager: Anna Oler

Library of Congress Cataloging-in-Publication Data

Plumly, Stanley.
Orphan hours : poems / Stanley Plumly. — 1st ed.
p. cm.
ISBN 978-0-393-07664-6
I. Title.
PS3566.L78O76 2012
811'.54—dc23

2012008185

W. W. Norton & Company, Inc.
500 Fifth Avenue, New York, N.Y. 10110
www.wwnorton.com

W. W. Norton & Company Ltd.
Castle House, 75/76 Wells Street, London W1T 3QT

1 2 3 4 5 6 7 8 9 0

for Michael Collier

Jan 1. 1821
~~*Hours hours*~~
~~*Pale cold*~~ *Orphan hours*

— SHELLEY

Contents

Lapsed Meadows   17

The Crows at 3 A.M.   18

The Jay   21

My Lawrence   23

Cancer   26

Lost Key   28

On Deciding Not to Be Buried
    but Burned   35

Four Hundred Mourners   37

Look for Me   39

Verisimilitude   41

Glenn Gould   42

Cello   43

Umberto D.   45

The Best Years of Our Lives   47

Vesper Sparrow   50

Afterward   52

Wistman's Wood   54

On Dartmoor   56

Arbitrarily   59

Perspective 61

Blind 63

Ground Birds in Open Country 66

Amidon Christmas Tree
    Farm Cardinal 68

I Love You 70

Sitting Alone in the Middle
    of the Night 71

John 20 72

Dayton 75

Nature 80

Nurture 82

As Reported 84

The Day of the Failure in Saigon,
    Thousands in the Streets, Hundreds
    Killed, A Lucky Few Hanging On the
    Runners of Evacuating Copters 86

Black Walnuts 88

From the Window of the Quiet Car 90

The Sand 92

Canto XVIII 94

Imaginary Prisons 99

Human Excrement 100

Caravaggio's *Conversion* 101

At Seventy-one 102

Orphan Hours 103

Dusk Coming On Outside
    _____, New York 106

The Lost Wine   107
On the Beach at Duck   108
On the Lawn at the Forians   109
Leavings   110

Dedications   111

Acknowledgments

Thanks are due the editors of the following magazines in which poems in this volume were originally published, many of which have undergone—sometimes radical—revision.

The American Poetry Review, Antaeus, The Atlantic, Connotation Press, The Gettysburg Review, Gulf Coast, Harvard Review, Hayden's Ferry Review, The Hopkins Review, The Kenyon Review, The New Republic, The New Yorker, The Ohio Review, and *Poetry Northwest.*

"Nurture": Some of the found material in this poem is drawn from the Venerable Bede's *Ecclesiastical History of the English People* (Book II, Chapter XIII), Penguin Classics, Revised Edition, 1991; and from William Wordsworth's *Two-Part Prelude* (Part I), W. W. Norton, 1970.

"As Reported": Paraphrase and quotations are from Jonathan Franzen's "Emptying the Skies," *The New Yorker,* July 26, 2010.

"Canto XVIII": originally published, in different form, in *Dante's Inferno: Translations by 20 Contemporary Poets,* ed. Daniel Halpern, Ecco, 1993.

"Human Excrement" and "Dusk Coming On Outside
_____, New York" first appeared, in different
form, in *Poems for a Small Planet: Contemporary American
Nature Poetry,* eds. Robert Pack and Jay Parini, University of
New England Press, 1993.

"The Lost Wine" is freely adapted from Paul Valéry's "Le
Vin Perdu," *Poésies,* Gallimard, 1942.

Versions of "Ground Birds in Open Country" and "Veri-
similitude" appeared as broadsides designed by Michael
Kaylor and Richard Russell respectively.

The epigraph is from one of Shelley's *Notebook* entries
among the Bodleian Shelley Manuscripts as quoted in Ann
Wroe's remarkable biography *Being Shelley: The Poet's Search
for Himself,* Pantheon, 2007.

Appreciation to Lindsay Bernal for the preparation of the
manuscript. And to the University of Maryland whose sup-
port made completion of this book possible.

Orphan Hours

Lapsed Meadows

Wild has its skills. The apple grew so close
to the ground it seemed the tree was thicket,
crab, and root, and by fall would look like brush
among the burdock and the hawkweed, as if at heart
it had been cut and piled for burning.
Along the edges, at the corners, like failed fence,
the hawthorns, by comparison, seemed planted.
Everywhere else there was broom grass, timothy,
and wood fern, and sometimes a sapling,
sometimes a run of hazel; sometimes, depending,
fruit still green or grounded and rotting underfoot.
I remember, in Ohio, fields of wastes of nature,
lost pasture, fallow clearings, buckwheat
and fireweed and broken sparrow nests,
especially in the summer, in the fading hilltop sun,
when you could lose yourself by simply lying down.
Who will find you, who will call you home now, at dusk,
with the dry tips of the goldenrod confused
with a little wind, filling in what's left of the light?

The Crows at 3 A.M.

The politically correct, perfect snow of Vermont
undulant under the lightly bruised, moonlit-backed-
becoming-storm-clouds slowing then speeding just
    above
the lines of blue spruce on Mount Mansfield here in
what I'm told is the state's "cloudiest county,"
vaguely an analogy for the plate tectonics of the blankets
constantly shifting from the left to the right side
of my body, pulling the heart, until by dawn I'm holding
    on,
waking with the cold, somehow looking at my hands
in the pearl dark that look like the first fall-castings
of the sycamore, those pocked dry leaves
that were my mother's final hands: sallow
dying coloring, mapping liverspots, rootlike
veining texturing the underdermal surfaces. The test,

writes Fitzgerald, in an essay called "The Crack-Up,"
of a first-rate intelligence is the ability to hold
opposing ideas in the mind at the same time yet retain
the ability to function. He couldn't, he says, so he
    cracked
like a plate. He is trying to update Keats's

notion of *"Negative Capability,* that is
when a man is capable of being in uncertainties,
Mysteries, doubts, without any irritable reaching after
    fact
& reason—Coleridge, for instance, would let go
by a fine isolated verisimilitude
caught from the Penetralium of mystery,
from being incapable of remaining content with
    half-knowledge."
When I heard the crows, like raven-geese, rending the
    dark,
filling the falling snow with wings,

                            I thought, for a moment,
they were speaking or singing.
Crows at the hour—Fitzgerald again—of "a dark night
of the soul," Poe-like crows chasing back and forth
in a quandary or a quarrel, up and down the Gihon.
Then they disappeared, let me drift back into sleep
to find my hands holding my mother's hands as if to help
    her
rise from the cold dead dream light of Vermont.
Stevens' twenty or so blackbirds may differ in their scale,
but their beauty of inflections and innuendoes
is no less present in the settled order,
passing out of hearing, out of sight. Thus the river's
    moving,
the blackbird must be flying, two half knowledges

or halves of one knowing. Those who love us who now
    live
in the air live in a loneliness we can only imagine.

The Jay

He does not lie there remembering
the blue-jay, say the jay.

　　　　　—STEVENS

In white Adirondack chairs, on the wave-crest of a dune,
looking out over the gray-green-to-cobalt-colder-blue
of the Atlantic, drinking decadence in large Barolo
portions, taking in, like sea-air, the view and ocean
silence, it's difficult to imagine not being here,
or, worse, never being here again, or, worse, never
having been here. My mother never saw an ocean,
and Wallace Stevens never traveled except by Pullman
to Key West and all the stops between. He speaks,
in "Madame La Fleurie," of his mother as the raven
"waiting parent," though mother also means the earth,
welcoming the child back to the beginning and end.

Naturally the sun is falling, which had risen in first
light only this morning, burning its stunning star-path
perfect to this place of witness. Now that it's a rose
disintegrating, in all the colors of the spectrum
all at once, we can look at it the way it is, on fire.
The way, too, the big male of a blue jay on the snow fence

to the right, watching with us, waits for the dark
or what passes for the dark, a kind of water-surface blue,
and the second the sun is gone he's gone just over us,
a few feet at the most, likely into the safety of a hedge.
We'd been imagining the need to recognize the
     moment's
moment before it disappears, as if you could know

a thing before it happens, life in the future tense,
when, in fact, like sunlight on the water here and there,
we live in one time but think in another. We were,
if not exactly, close to drunk, so we lifted to the light
our full glasses. The jay was beautiful. Especially
in the air, blue on blue, his white wing-spots and white
touch on the tail shining in that instant of the sun
slipping under. Not once, in his happiness or reverence
or indifference, did he sing, complain, or say anything.
He flew on a line drawn in time from now to then.
I can still see him, though finally he was nothing
but a blur inside the death of everything that happens.

My Lawrence

The future, rain in every syllable and cell,
comes home later and later, until it's half past
morning and time to go to work all over again.
David Herbert Lawrence's collier father working
his way toward death in little pieces—I could see
him in the book as I could hear my own breaking
into the house in the dead middle of the night.
Work requires a ton and then a lump of coal to build up
fires like a setting sun you look at and call nature,
beautiful furnace fires that turn back flesh
to smoke and ash, back to the drift and ghost
it comes from. Read everything, the English teachers
said—I read Lawrence first at a big oak dining table
in a Quaker reading room, though not, I think,
the novels but something more like *Studies in
Classic American Literature,* literature abridged
sometimes for children, which Lawrence takes seriously:
Irving's bowling Dutchmen, Cooper's noble savages,
Poe's still living dead, Melville's South Sea natives
and God in a white whale's head, even Hawthorne's
scarlet letter worn as a final warning in a fundamental
Boston surrounded by the trees—brilliant analyses,
written like short stories, stories like his poems

or his strange travel essays or his blood-dark
archetypal fiction, memory when memory fails.
Thus his imagined father in firelight at the fireplace,
having at that moment the overwhelming thought
that this is what his life has come to, a passage
between impossibilities, morning and evening, climbing
the ladder into the earth, climbing the ladder back.
Sons and Lovers, sons and fathers, children's stories—
by the time I got to Paul Morel, the Bottoms and Hell
    Row
and the tiny, bricky, garden-patched rowhouses, now
    part
of "Greater Nottingham," got there literally, too,
early in the sixties, in search of where he started,
before his own search for self sent him to Australia,
America, and Italy, I thought I understood how much
we feel alone in the company of fathers, how work itself
is a father: the scene in *Women in Love* when Gerald
    Crich
dives to save his sister and her lover, who lie
in an embrace at the bottom of a pond, among a living
    world
of mud and growth and stone, dives again and again. . . .
Crich walks finally out of the water covered, alone,
and says there's room for thousands down there.
His father, who would own life and death, either weeps
or tries to strike him or, in the density of prose,
does both. Then coal dust, or something vaguely like it,

veiling the autumn air of a Turner English twilight.
I remember standing cold outside his childhood home.
It was raining and no one knew who Lawrence was.

Cancer

Mine, I know, started at a distance
five hundred and twenty light-years away
and fell as stardust into my sleeping mouth,
yesterday, at birth, or that time when I was ten
lying on my back looking up at the cluster
called the Beehive or by its other name
in the constellation Cancer,
the Crab, able to move its nebulae projections
backward and forward, side to side,
in the tumor Hippocrates describes as carcinoma,
from *karkinos,* the analogue, in order to show
what being cancer looks like.
Star, therefore, to start,
like waking on the best day of your life
to feel this living and immortal thing inside you.
You were in love, you were a saint,
you were going to walk the sunlight blessing water,
you were almost word for word forever.
The crown, the throne, the thorn—
now to see the smoke shining in the mirror,
the long half dark of dark down the hallway inside it.
Now to see what wasn't seen before:
the old loved landscape fading from the window,
the druid soul within the dying tree,

the depth of blue coloring the cornflower,
the birthday-ribbon river of a road,
and the young man who resembles you
opening a door in the half-built house
you helped your father build,
saying, in your voice, come forth.

Lost Key

—A woman I saw once through her basement
apartment window, in London, in the sixties,
sitting in the Buddha position on the floor
with her evening meal in front of her, cast
in the cadaverous blue-green glow of a TV screen:
I can't say why, after decades, this stays with me,
except that at the time I couldn't read the passive
look of peace yet anger on her face, distorted
in the fish-light, though I saw her again,
just days ago, as a woman in the full-length
of a window in a brownstone walking toward me
as if to speak or break the glass, all of it
so fast I couldn't tell.

                    —Signs and wonders.
My mother would sit for hours inside silence,
who also loved windows and the picture
of the world outside them, especially those
distances that start out, in Ohio, as fields
unmarked with fences, here and there the big oaks
witnessing the planting, or later, towering
in the snow piling up in waves against the rails
not far enough and too far away. When she read
her tragic books her mind, too, went away

on a long train passing, passengers inside,
her solitude the life she imagined she could see
as she put down the page and closed her eyes.

—Jamie claimed it had flown into her hand
when, in fact, it had landed on her shoulder.
In Louisiana, where small birds drink from cups
of the live oak leaves, people have a gift of voice
songbirds recognize. She brought it home,
a sparrow of some kind, up and down the stairs,
off and on her shoulder, within its living cage.
It behaved like a bird you can buy, listening
and answering the talk, walking all the fingers,
and outside sometimes flying, flying back,
circling the playground like a toy,
until a day it didn't, when all the other birds
just like it came to visit.

                                        —In the story
of the jinnee, the soul is a sparrow hidden
in a box hidden in another, diminishing to seven,
diminished even further in seven smaller chests
hidden "in a coffer of marble," with the captive
placed in covenant, to be hidden in a cave
"within the verge of the circumambient ocean,"
only to be discovered, the sparrow strangled.
Or is the soul the raindrop as it falls back
to the sea or the single star stationed in Orion?
Rhetorical compared to the thrush's evensong,

the beauty of the redwing, and the living soul
about to leave the mouth, moth then butterfly.

—And what is the season in heaven, given
Carrara marble clouds, blue robin's egg-shell walls,
sunlight in the rain? On earth we say a tree
is evergreen, its conical-needle changes changing
nothing of its constancy, though even thousand-
year-old pines fail a little more each year.
The man died or the man didn't die,
the difference like a candle's breath of flame
a door too quickly closed or opened could easily
blow out. Waxwings, firebirds in the hundreds,
fill the ladders of green branches, climb
then scale the almost-out-of-sight, and join
the color in the sky only ultimately visible.

—We look to the clouds, after all. Constable,
in a summer of his grief, decides that clouds
are where grief lives, cumulonimbus-sized
cathedrals building and unbuilding in order
to stay afloat above the grave that is the earth.
He draws by brush on paper wet as rain,
as if by painting clouds his dying wife's frail
health will find a healing place transcendent.
He works within his Hampstead garden hours,
abstracted in the sky, creating, by example,
life after death . . . old hours that acquire,

accumulate, and rise, forming and reforming,
like the paintings, all that water, air can hold.

—A part of nature, a lapsed fall meadow,
thistle, vetch, and yarrow gone to pasture shades
of mullein (Quaker rouge), mustard, and white aster,
a language of long parallels, the way, in Dutch,
thistle is *distel,* "something sharp," the national
flower of Scotland, though the tallest sample
I've ever seen is Umbrian, six feet or more,
pulling all its water up from stone to floral crown,
a pale plum damson, like the blush of sex. . . .
We were driving from central Rome to coastal Fano,
toward the flat Adriatic, the terrain built of rock
on rock cut by rivers pouring down the elevations,
once in a while the rose of a thistle bursting.

—The narrative depending on who's telling.
I lost a small key, the size of a penny
or a fingerprint (a mailbox key), and I hate
to think how upset I was, less for the key's simple
function than for the confusions keys organize against.
Like the hairline fracture in marble or my mother's
half-moon scar, I thought it meant something:
an overlove of order or a special need for seasons.
I thought the lost key was telling me to leave,
and in increments so small I'd have to dream them
to see them, the way, in anticipation of losses,

we make a duplicate, a copy just in case.
The night my mother died she held on to me

in order to keep her body upright over depths
above which lying down means falling.
Outside, the crystal skeletal snow was falling,
while in the wind that starts from the ground
it would suddenly rise. The sky was nothing,
but fifteen floors below carlights under the streetlights
slowed, then midnight into early morning passed,
and windows seemed so sheer they opened on the cold.
Air in the room was glistening, yet her gray eyes
kept their clarity and her three-quarters-of-a-century
face its comprehension. Air, she said, was the angel.
Outside, the white constructions of the snow,
building at different speeds, falling from different

heights, replaced the shapes of things with ghosts:
her snow-covered hands holding fast to the fear
that she was alone and without death would end
as one of those women on the street
who in weather sleeps wrapped up in cars.
My mother's poverty, her soft hand on a forehead
still prone to fever and a childhood fear of ceilings.
If I fall asleep still half-awake, someone in
a half voice is talking. What is she saying,
what is she saying? Who remembers sleeping, anyway,
save for the waking and what we call rising,

returning from a dream we thought we had
but can't quite put together?

        —Those rich Sunday walks,
London, Maida Vale, straight on up through St. John's
Wood to Chalk Farm Road and Belsize Park to
   Hampstead,
hoping to meet John Keats: walking the one good thing
to clear the head. Sometimes I went straight south,
Edgware Road through Hyde Park and the Gardens,
to Kensington and Chelsea and Cheyne Walk,
where Whistler walked, planning his night boat rides
along the Thames, doing his memory work, looking
for the shades and lights of shadows reflected off
the water, complaining, if the sky was near,
of too many stars, too much to remember
to take home with him.

        —Water and its wine
turned into blood, bread of the body.
Who can trust in these except to love the dead?
Flesh back into word, like the spirit in the dry wood
rising from the fire, channeling the airy brightness.
What I saw in the sky each day for a year, for seventy
years, in truth, was never the same, never the same,
not the fixed stars moving in rotation nor the one
moon in its variety. I watched, each fall,
the infinite leaf change and disappear, held it

in my hand, watched it curl, turn to paper,
blow away, never the same, in the same way as words:
to leave, to go or flower, never both at once.

—I lift what I think is a sweet Dolcetto,
which stains the sunlight sleeping on the air.
I break the bread seasoned with rosemary. These,
in themselves, miracles. I think what I'll see
through the glass will be nothing but a face
at last made visible: and what I'll hear
is what's been said forgotten. No wonder death
is stone blind, sealed lips, and beyond recognition.
No wonder words are wasted breath.
I saw a woman in a London flat sitting on the floor,
between worlds, in the Buddha position.
I saw her again, a lifetime since, walking toward me
into the full-length frame of a window, one of us alive.

On Deciding Not to Be Buried
but Burned

When the lawyer asked I thought the options through,
not that there were many, then decided, like the
　　majority,
to end up underground in order to assume my throne in
　　heaven.
But later, and in love, the truth about my body bothered
　　me,
the way gravity, another word for *grave,* had taken
　　over—
pull of the earth, moon tides, reformation of the stars,
leaf by leaf the dying heart alive inside its bell,
my parents lying side by side beside their parents—
while the mind wanted nothing more than early
　　mornings,
early evenings of the doves in the live oaks they sing in
and fly from, lifting, turning, circling back to home:
it wanted clarity, stone shadow, the bright air water blue,
to see the mile of the animal still moving on the hill,
to lie down in the grass and rest and wake up free
from tasks, especially remembering: though I
　　remembered

things I'd touched, small things, things they place in
    pockets
or your hands—letters, wedding rings, photographs so
    dated
no one but the ghosts knows where or who from
    whom—the kinds
of things you keep in drawers until the day someone
    finds them,
hopes they matter in the afterlife, along with pyx and
    cups
and golden bread and the wine's Lacrima Christi. That's
when I knew that when the time came that what was left
    of me,
especially memory, had to be purged, forgotten in a fire.

Four Hundred Mourners

The sizes of the crowds in those burn-baby-burn days
were at best estimates, depending on who—
the police, the press, the thousands in protest—
was counting. The body count, we called it,
and after the arrest we were lined up
alphabetically for fingerprints and phone calls.
It wasn't all that much, though the numbers
made a difference since they argued significance.
That was later, at the dead end of the sixties,
the rallies against the war mixed with the killings
of the Kennedys and King and the nuclear meltdown
of democracy at the convention in Chicago.
But at the beginning of the decade
it was man-on-the-moon, hand-on-the-heart.
Ralph Abernathy, who had recruited most of us,
came by one day just to say hello.
We were on the white side of the table,
the soon-to-be-eligible black voters on the other.
Greenville was as liberal as it got in Mississippi,
the Delta almost as ancient as the flooding of the Nile.
The names, the spellings, the signatures,
like maps of a world once flat.
And the heat and the dog's-breath weight of the air
and the wet dust needlework of pine.

People had died here under a different register,
as thousands more thousands of nautical miles
southeast would die who had not voted.
Ralph said the numbers finally didn't matter,
the idea of change was enough.
He meant "an idea whose time has come."
The few new voters each seemed wise and old,
older than anyone we knew, older than parents
or grandparents, older than the country
or anger's life expectancy.
They had looked into the sun,
they had looked into it a long time.
The Carter family newspaper spoke of joy
with sometimes grief, as if the happiness
of change felt like a passage.
This is fifty years now, gone.
It's crazy that so much of it came back to me
witnessing the funeral of a child.
The countless car cortege wound through the town's
winter wastes as if the hearse could not quite find its
    way.
There is no end to the death of a child,
so that when we detoured past her elementary school
everyone was out in the cold, in the hundreds, waving.

Look for Me

If you want me again
look for me anywhere but here,
preferably out of the country, say, Italy,
up by the glacial lakes, among the ghostly Alps
and the green pre-Alps, in the shadow of Monte Rosa,
in one of the little towns, places I've lived,
in fact and memory, like Varenna or Laveno,
right there at the top lip of the water,
midnight at its depth, daylight breaking waves.
Or west, on a line, in the Piedmont, above Liguria,
where they grow the darkest grape, Nebbiolo,
between the villages of Alba and Barolo,
on a patch-and-rag landscape of dusky blue hillsides.
Or south, off the warm coast of Vesuvius,
islands like the goat crests of pale mountains.
Cities, too, the Paris of the 6th, off Saint-Suplice,
the walk-up second floor of a small boutique hotel,
in stone or stucco, especially near the corner
of rue Férou and rue de Vaugirard,
nothing I could afford except to run a bill.
Though Prague I could afford, at least for a while,
the Ministry of Education Residence on Dlouhá,
just down the street from the centuries-old
flat-iron-looking building where Kafka wrote

his *Metamorphosis* and various alleged prose poems
in order to fill an absence or a silence.
And if I were depressed, meaningfully depressed,
London, on a bus, the number 6, the upper deck,
waxing and waning Edgware Road to Marble Arch
then left on Oxford Street, with heads
of all the shoppers, block by block, bobbing
or slowly swimming by, death having undone so many.
And Princess Street, in winter, coal-covered stone,
monument on monument measuring its length,
the gray snow and grayer wind piling up the dry ice
in the air, driving it home, into the heart.
Places I've lived and would happily die in,
like homesick alien vertical Manhattan,
on a workday, among a million, drawing a crowd
and being celebrated, lying there alone with my one
soul looking up at the scraper-boxed-in sky,
with, off and on, storm clouds towering into heaven.
So much moving on, so much sitting still,
so much living time traveling
or watching through the seasons the split spilt oak
turn golddust on the lawn. Look for me
wherever and at last outside the empty house
invisible or visible, but there,
but only if you want me again.

Verisimilitude

Very similar, very simile—
a smile, a gesture, a mark on the air,
to wave hello, good-bye, to throw a kiss
across the rainbow distances. "The word love,"
writes syphilitic Paul Gauguin, in his journal in Tahiti,
"I'd like to kick whoever invented it in the teeth."
Gauguin the realist in paradise, painting
cinnamon women in native floral outlines
in real two dimensions, beautiful flat faces.
Then the counterargument: Plato's homely metaphor
of how, in our first life, we were whole,
male and female, but cut in half
by gods no less fearful than Gauguin,
the way we cut eggs in half with a hair,
the eggs hard-boiled, the hair the thread of a tailor.
When is a thing not like another thing,
like the split sweet heart of an apple?
We're so filled with absence,
or as Yeats, after Porphyry, puts it,
the "honey of generation," no wonder we stand
in the street at night, half or wholly drunk, shouting.

Glenn Gould

I heard him that one night in Cincinnati.
The concert hall, 1960, the same day
Kennedy flew into town in perfect sunlight
and rode the route that took him
through the crowds of voters and nonvoters
who alike seemed to want to climb
into the armored convertible.
Gould did not so much play as address
the piano from a height of inches,
as if he were trying to slow the music
by holding each note separately.
Later he would say he was tired
of making public appearances,
the repetition of performing the Variations
was killing him. But that night
Bach felt like a discovery, whose repetitions
Gould had practiced in such privacy
as to bring them into being for the first time.
This was the fall, October, when Ohio,
like almost every other part of the country,
is beginning to be mortally beautiful,
the great old hardwoods letting go
their various scarlet, yellow,
and leopard-spotted leaves one by one.

Cello

The one I saw onstage between the legs
of the obviously tall young woman
dressed in the dinner formal wear
of giving a solo concert
under what seemed a single klieg light,
her face, from a little distance,
apparently abstracted, eyes almost closed,
one white perfect arm semi-circling the instrument,
which, unlike what we sometimes have believed,
was not an extension of her body
but her partner, the music itself—
Bach's "Prelude in G Minor"—
yet another, a third thing, separate from the air.
I think it was the skirt slightly lifted
off the ankle while draped somehow
and up against the combination heartwood
of the spruce and silver maple
and her fingers on the fingerboard
moving as if tapping out a code
that made her art so palpable,
though I think from the elegant neckwork
down to the functional tailpiece
and pencil of an endpin
she was in such control

as to forget we were there.
Then the bow, horsehair and pernambuco,
like old love's aging arrow of longing—
caught midair by the artist's sleight of hand—
sent to draw our blood with a wounding
so severe as to leave no visible scar.

Umberto D.

Umberto Domenico Ferrari is waiting for a train
not to stop, hugging to his chest his mix of mutt
and spot-eyed Jack Russell, who has been faithful
as well as touched with charm, including the ability
to hold, while on its haunches, a felt hat in its mouth,
intended to be filled with paper money.
This is the day Umberto is evicted from his shabby
one-room residence for lack of payment, lack of funds,
lack of prospects altogether: a pensioner whose bed's
been rented by the hour whenever he walks Flike.
Neo-realism in the fifties means to imitate real life,
so Vittorio De Sica has selected from the world
Carlo Battisti, a pensioner himself and once-professor,
to take on the role of civil poverty in prewar
Mussolini Italy, in which, in black and white,
the sun is always pale, skin a bright gray pallor,
the air almost nothing to see through. Except
for the dog there's loneliness, the shelter, the hospice,
or the grave where Umberto could find a curl or corner,
become a member of the corps of the aging indigent.
Throughout the picture the slight orchestral score
has been barely audible, yet has echoed down
the cobbled streets and terra cotta walls
like orphan wind wandering the Campagnia,

underwear and shirts and flowery dresses
riffling on lines between high windows,
all of its long music inside Umberto's head
on his evening-long dog walks. He must make a choice.
De Sica has photographed the story no comment,
as if the natural light of Rome were neutral,
like the pregnant servant girl, Umberto's other friend,
who isn't sure and may not care who the father is,
or like Umberto's enemy, his platinum looming
    landlady,
a kind of mix herself of opera and brothel.
This is the war already, Umberto and the women
its home soldiers. And this the day the saved loved dog
is walked to a sort of orphanage for dogs: killers,
whiners, lungers, dogs in dog purgatory. "I'll bet he's
feisty," the purgatory keeper says, one hand on the leash,
the other on the money. In real life, cinéma vérité,
we end as children or finally human or animal anima.
Umberto must make a choice, which is to stand
with Flike embraced in front of a train,
one of those that moves so fast just standing close
takes your breath away. The dog breaks free.
And for a moment Umberto is alone among the dead,
then suddenly alive again, Flike again, and play.

The Best Years of Our Lives

What in Hollywood is called a throw-away line,
the line Virginia Mayo delivers into the mirror
as she's turning from fixing her hair to tell
the now-civilian, out-of-work Dana Andrews,
in case he hasn't already received the message,
that she wants a divorce, that she's given him
the best years of her life, which in truth
amount to no more than six months, since the war
has used up most of the time of their marriage.
All the while the next man, Steve Cochran,
another veteran, is waiting in the lobby
of the two rooms, small kitchen, and a bath.
Andrews, anyway, loves someone else, Fredric
March's and Myrna Loy's daughter, the woman
every woman in the audience admires, even if
she's second in the order of virtue to the girl
the boy who's lost his hands in battle loves,
the girl next door, who's waited at the window
as Cathy O'Donnell playing to perfection love.
Everyone in the picture is a veteran of some kind.
What's amazing is that it's less than a year
after the war that the picture's been made,
a story of homecoming, of surviving change,
of what a generation, not so different from

the Lost, has come through, which may be why
my mother, sitting in the bandbox of Piqua's
Little Theater, in nineteen forty-eight, two
years later than the film's first release,
because nothing seems to arrive on time in Ohio,
is crying—she's on my left in a torn seat
in tears and has been from the opening credits.
I'm nine, and we're a pair, movies once a week
our one night out, my father at the front doors
taking tickets to earn what he can't cutting
lumber. The wisdom of being nine is knowing
feelings, and I can feel something on the screen
pouring out inside the cone of light above our
heads and falling on all of us and through us,
scattered in the space here and there, as if
what we're seeing is more than what we're seeing.
It's hours before the picture ends, hopeful,
with a wedding, the kind of hope, I realize
in my wisdom, adults can't live without, though
my favorite part has less to do with love
than with the cockpit of the B-17 lined up
for junk with hundreds, row on row, like the one
Andrews used to fly in and is inspired to climb
inside again to reminisce the nightmare. He's
come here to these fields that will be suburbs
looking, like my father, for a job, yet finds
himself sitting in the bubble of a bomber,
its glass a net of scars, with the sky-borne
camera and the Friedhofer score bearing down

on him, until the full-on shot shifts like
an assassin coming from behind to show how
vulnerable and like a child he is, but blessed,
at last, by sunlight and the future. It's
a scene to break your heart, so many are.
The lumber my father cut that year almost built
our house, half in the country, half in town.
And he won a car, a Chevy, that he and my mother
drove into another car, and walked away from whole.

Vesper Sparrow

Said and done I'm choosing the redwing.
The unwritten rule is the rule of familiars,
the mocker in the arbor picking at the grapes,
the house wren flowering in the dogwood,
the catbird mewling in and out of the hedge,
the infinite warbler warbling all summer. . . .
But not the bird you feed all winter,
the one who stays, like the sometimes cardinal,
who warms the snow at the window,
who on the coldest day will sing,
since singing, by itself, like beauty, is nothing,
is what the birdwatching world longed for.
Nor does the lyric thrush, brown as a fall oak leaf,
    qualify,
since death wants black and only a little color.
Thus jays are equally pointless because obvious,
their blue blood, like a fresh wound, too bright.
Nor will the minion sparrow do, smaller than the thrush
and no less common, plain as bread or prayer.
Yet she claimed for her own, once, vesper sparrows—
their treetop dexterity, their clear ascending
and descending flight song—then later changed her
    mind.
She, too, wanted something darker, with color,

redstart or starling or blue-black purple martin,
something in the evening light disappearing.
Those of us who'll wish at last for redwings
want the yellow of the sun under the heart's blood
on each wing in measure just enough to remind us
of where we've come from, the way the blackbird
    opening
to fly brings back word from the old life to the new.

Afterward

Sometimes, for all time, we just tire of the struggle,
of what Stevens calls "the celestial ennui of apartments,"
from the umpteenth floor looking down through the
    ultimate
open window. A young man I knew, full of promise,
but filled, even more, with an emptiness he couldn't
comprehend, took the elevator one night to the top
of his father's Manhattan building, stepped out
onto the balcony of his father's living room,
and like an Icarus drawn to the dark side of the moon
flew from this world. Who hasn't had trouble,
especially at the edge, looking down into the heart
of the air, its depthlessness and purity?
Nor need we climb dream ladders to look down.
In the eyes of the other the pigment of the color
will sometimes separate, like snow, each fleck or flake
the paler version of itself falling, melting.
On Wednesday the king died, on Friday the queen
    died—
or is it the reverse?—E. M. Forster's definition
of narrative, and his idea of plot,
the fact that the queen dies of grief.
Causes and their effects, the romance
that halfway down or at the end we're saved.

What or who she saw at the bottom of her fall
matters less than the weight of pain she carried there—
and all that practice running the stadium stairs
in order to disguise the looking-down,
if only to wonder, time after time, at the distance.

Wistman's Wood

More like a witches' wood, a patch of acreage
halfway up the hill above West Dart,
a moorland stream you can almost step across,
but clear, fast, as if it were descending off a mountain.
The wood, too, descending as if sliding, though that
    aspect
of its attitude is wind, blowing, like the river,
west to east, so constant in its quest
it blows away the birds and cuts in half the trees—
stunted primal oaks, deities, enchantresses,
anomalies of spirits underground, or are they,
these isolated, ancient, broken beings,
like me, bent in the middle of their souls?

Because it matters, imagine Wistman's Wood
for what it is, centuries, perpetual,
growing out of stone at human height, limestone
big as boulders, all of it locked up in Devon mist
and barnacled with lichen. We were there in winter.
We were warned. The path between the bogs
and floating marsh was far too small to tolerate
    mistakes,
and the signs said so. It took an hour or more
walking single file from where we left the car

at the crossroads at Two Bridges.
Were we happy, were we ever going to die?
I should have held your hand, and then held on.

On Dartmoor

Even at a distance it looks old, older than old—an extended island of three consecutive copses of swaybacked English oak the color of stone. Closer up, at walking speed, the enclosures, like ancient pillaged castle walls, begin to flow into one another, with the undergrowth and giant clitter forming the transitions between larger structures. Then when you are almost close enough to touch it the whole thing looms and unifies, suddenly undifferentiated, simultaneous.

That is when the singular plural of the noun really kicks in: when you are at the broken wall of the wood and can begin to appreciate, even absorb, its opacity, its confusion, and can, once your eyes focus on distinctions, begin to separate one tree from another.

Wistman's Wood is both one tree and multiples of that one, whose trunk and lateral branching is layered with centuries of secondary life—vines and vegetation— and whose root system, like an afterthought of itself, is rooted in stone, which is also gray green with erosion and encrustation. One fundamental tree, one fundamental stone, with mirrors.

But this is no primitive rain forest. In its thickness and intimacy and low-doorway height it is medieval, a fantasy of sorcery, a primary human space mysteriously abandoned, alive with age. Its primacy and continuity and modesty are naturally connected, since as an entity the wood seems to have accepted, from the outset, its limitations.

Rather than trying to reach too high or too far in any one direction, rather than trying to assume territory or increase of its numbers, rather than acting like a forest—which it profoundly is not—it has achieved a kind of immortality or self-perpetuation through an internal and necessary understanding of its special place on the landscape, its special configuration within the weather, which can be extreme, and its especial knowledge of the wind, which is constant. It is like a great old architectural event from out of the deep past, haunted by survival.

This is a wood of trees in the middle of a landmass sea, with a variable sea wind, facts that not only discipline the expansion of the wood's margins but help shape its actual vertical growth. It is as if the wood were at the ocean's edge, with the wind always landward. Out of resistance, therefore, the trees, an acreage of them, are bent, from west to east, at a height of ten to fifteen feet—angles that are further emphasized by the angle of the eastern incline of the valley they grow out of.

As it pours down the opposite side of West Dart Valley and crosses the ribbon of the West Dart River, the wind seems to pick up power with the potential of a wave. This is a Dartmoor wind, from across the ocean cliff faces and open distances of Cornwall and Devon.

No wonder the branches elongate on a line parallel with the earth until their weight forces them back toward the tips of their roots. Among such trees there can be no lift toward the theology of the sky, no possibility of ascension.

The wind, as the most active and visible agent of change on the moor, drives the branches downward and inward toward the wreck of the granite, lichen-covered boulders the trees seem to cling to. Tangled as they are—branch returning to root—and hoisted out of the warping angles of the stones, the tree-shapes suggest any number of things, not the least of which is a cloister, a series of cloisters, or interiors, where the voice of the wind is the spirit in the wood.

Arbitrarily

Death, I've decided, is gray,
and for me at least not the Raphaelean angel gray of
    doves,
nor the "gray-brown" hermit gray of Whitman's thrush,
nor the nettle in the hedge or neutral garden thorn,
nor the English grey of lawns
leading to the limestone grey of Bridesheads,
though I love such examples of monotone and texture,
yet none of them the gray of the mining gray of
    Philipsburg,
the silver in the ground,
or the asphalt gray of parking lots
drifting coast to coast, sea to shining sea, ocean to gray
    ocean,
or the nickel-diming rain that starts each morning
in the past and fills the day.
The remnant dressed in black, the bride in white—
I saw them more than once and knew the circle
of their color a gray nowhere in nature,
unless the wind or breath-of-life or air walled-in
suggests a gray interior in things, the way we see it
in the mirror manifest in hair and one-time lyric of the
    face,
the changes imperceptible but there, the same warm look

of ash turning into smoke, though heavy, like a leaf.
Like leaves of pages in my mother's favorite books,
their gray-on-gray the substance of the shadings of the
    soul,
souls like Emma Bovary and Anna Karenina
and other country girls who marry to be safe
then kill themselves,
women of the century,
who understand how gray is like a cancer nothing cures.
Even language, written down, is black on white,
a stay against the moment's god oblivion
and the soft gray earth under the hard gray stone,
gray the gravity we'll see in the camera of the eye
between life and death, the photograph a spirit flesh and
    blood,
something like a smear of egg and sperm
studied through a lens.
My thoughtful babysister in her Sunday special dress,
her eyes half closed to filter out the sun—
I'm thinking, too, beside her, leaning on a doorway,
my childish hand a shadow at my head.
Nineteen forty-four, our uncles in the war, gray
    gabardine.
My sister will outlive me in that dress,
who one day posed a picture thin as air.
We think the light is blinding. It is failing.

Perspective

Margaret says it's nothing more than perspective.
She's right, of course: perspective
being "the art of delineating solid objects
upon a plane surface so as to produce
the same impression of relative positions
and magnitudes, or of distance, as the actual objects
do when viewed from a particular point"
(Oxford Standard), the point
being the full and light-filled moon looked at,
here in mid-October, from the perspective of walking
    away from it
down Beacon Court. Perspective was what I lacked
an ability with when I was an art student
trying to sight down the row of different-storied
buildings on the far side of the street,
each one distinct yet connected,
as in a Hopper or Utrillo,
sun shadow or pencil-marking rain. Night, though,
is another thing altogether.
I'd just turned to consider
the blue cloud passing like a floating island nation
on the opposite end of the sky, then
turned back only to realize how high the moon had
    traveled,

had, in no time, risen as if lifted.
Perspective, Margaret said: like the problem I had
    drawing
depth of field, the illusion of a line diminishing
(the famous looming stones of graves in Queens
foreshadowing the skyline in Manhattan),
since perspective is as much about
the imagination as it is about
Brunelleschi.
As memory,
too, like too much in our lives, is perspective,
and between now and then often all we have.
Those, for instance, whom we've loved and unloved,
forming a line behind us, eventually fade,
in the long century photograph,
to the size of children or the half
of half of nothing of what they were.
I don't have the answer.
Come close, we say, but keep your distance
(as if perspective were a dance).
And as you walk away you'll disappear
(as if you'd not existed, were never here).

Blind

Out of the corner of the eye
(though cornea is more accurate),
a sudden pulse, a cut of color,
an electric sparkle of blood to the right
(though it's less in the eye than in the air
at the edge), the peripheral, sidelong,
slightly sidereal view, as if a star
the size of a flake of snow had fallen there
the second you move your head to tie your shoe.

It's the tired eye, the one that worked the dark
like a candle. So tired it wants to sleep
all by itself, roll back into "the fat
of the orbit," the sparkle the warning
the crystalline lens has slipped. On the list
of the one-eyed, eyes that never rest:
the eye of the needle, the potato, the storm,
the insomniac eye of the Cyclops,
the Egyptian eye of the pyramid.

Then the separated eye, like a sunny egg,
floating in its fluid. And the black eye,
the red eye, eye for I: "I, too," writes Whitman,
"lived . . . I, too, many and many a time

cross'd the river of old . . . Had my eyes
dazzled by the shimmering track of beams, /
Look'd at the fine centrifugal spokes of light
round the shape of my head in the sunlit water."
The double iris the way the spectrum

of light is changed, the multiple rainbow,
the regal florentina, the messenger of color,
the "thin, circular-shaped, contractile curtain,"
the poetry of the eye, this right eye of mine
stabbed by light that left the sun
eight minutes ago, that equally stabs
my friend John's corneal degeneration,
who reads Henry James through a glass darkly
and sees with vision brailled as twilight,

the iris aqueous behind the seeing surface,
blue and green and vague as the ocean.
Is the white eye of the moon blind
or does it see in part and sequence through its
cycle or is it only, like our own eyes, sunlight?
My mother's blindness beginning in her feet,
rising for years through her circulatory system,
blinding, finally, first her broken heart,
next her treble tongue, then her troubled mind,

and at the level of the eye's "capsule of Tenon"
killing the nerve ends, the feathery pink vessels,
her hand in the air straight ahead of her.

I think it's the sight of her I see
on the right peripheral side when I see
at the edge of the light the pulse of blood
or the icy voice of the tip of a knife refracting—
something like not seeing. Blind-sided.
Blind cornea, blind choroid, ciliary body, retina.

The blind couple I followed once, in Brookline,
down Winthrop to the Square, dead winter, with
a wind, the concretion of the snow piled head-high
at the corners, the early morning sidewalk
running slick, she, holding his hand, marking
the path out with her cane, he, her father
or her lover, knowing when to stop, where to wait,
the T, at last, arriving with its noise . . .
I watched them take their time getting on.

Ground Birds in Open Country

They fly up in front of you so suddenly,
tossed, like gravel, by the handful,
kicked like snow or dead leaves into life.
Or if it's spring they break back and forth
like schools of fish silver at the surface,
like the swifts I saw in the hundreds
over the red tile roofs of Assisi—
they made shadows, they changed sunlight,
and at evening, before vespers,
waved back to the blackbird nuns.
My life list is one bird at a time long,
what Roethke calls *looking*. The eye,
particular for color, remembers when
a treeful would go gray with applause,
in the middle of nowhere, in a one-oak field.
I clapped my hands just for the company.
As one lonely morning, green under glass,
a redwing flew straight at me, its shoulders
slick with rain that hadn't fallen yet.
In the birdbook there, where the names are,
it's always May, and the thing so fixed
we can see it—Cerulean, Blackpoll, Pine.
The time one got into the schoolroom
we didn't know what it was, but it sang,

it sailed along the ceiling on all sides,
and blew back out, wild, still lost,
before any of us, stunned, could shout
it down. And in a hallway once,
a bird went mad, window by locked window,
the hollow echo length of a building.
I picked it up closed inside my hand.
I picked it up and tried to let it go.
They fly up so quickly in front of you,
without names, in the slurred shapes of wings.
Scatter as if shot from twelve-gauge guns.
Or they fly from room to room, from memory
past the future, having already gathered
                in great numbers on the ground.

Amidon Christmas Tree Farm Cardinal

Already, before dawn, the calendar cold moon
still clear, sparkle of ice here and there,
and almost out of hearing, he is singing,
which is really, likely, countersinging,
interspersed with chip-calls, then for a while,
except for the hilltop wind riffling
the white-laced pines, silence,
as if he's disappeared through a door
left open in the air.

                    Yet by noon
his first-blood brilliant coloring is fire
against the snow, skilled in the way it moves,
with one side of his body tilted up,
one wing pointed in a signature of flight
(one wing tucked in tight)
in what the watchers call "lopsided pose,"
on a slip of branch outside the window
where he waits out the moment to reattack
the sunlight in the glass, which is striking
at an angle from some ninety million miles.

Now I watch him climb the storm frame
and say again his reasons,

                        watch him in a detail
impossible otherwise (his several criminal reds,
his flared sunlit crown, the bandit mask
that sets apart the quickness of his eyes),
so it's easy, when his mate shows up
and he shows off his bright head turning sideways,
to see just how he tips his tail and places
a piece of pine seed into her willing mouth.
She, too, one winter, flew at the glass.

I Love You

Death is at least the weight of what a day
adds up to. First the sun rising out of the blue,
turning into light through the warm afternoon,
then falling, an inch at a time, back into fire.
The moon, too, lighter than air, drifting through
the clouds with death's face on it. And stars,
count them, time running out. I love you,
a fact of life diurnal death despairs. At the end
of the day sleep reminds us of what it could be
like lying there. Waking is a way to remember
dreaming and dreaming a way to remember life.
The days, count them, are the one day over and over.
I lie there sometimes half-awake. Death, in that
moment, on the other side of me, is dreaming.

Sitting Alone in
the Middle of the Night

Maybe it was summer and I was back home for a while
working to pay off debts from school, painting white
barns and long field fences and on off-days baling hay.
It was hot then in Ohio and sometimes so dry the corn
or the soybeans would fail. I'd get up at two or three
in the morning to find my way to the kitchen for water
and he'd be sitting there in a kind of outline,
smoking and staring at something far, his eyes by now
long adjusted to the dark. Mine were just now opening.
Nothing would be said, since there was nothing to say.
He was dying, he was turning into stone. The little
I could see I could see already how much heavier
he made the air, heavy enough over the days that
    summer
you could feel in the house the pull of the earth.

John 20

When is the first day of the week
or the third day from Friday?
Mary Magdelene arrives Sunday at the sepulchre
so early it is dark but light enough to see the stone is
    gone,
and runs to find Peter and the other loved disciple
to tell them they—whoever they are—have taken his
    body
and we know not where they have laid him.
Who is the other disciple, who are we, who the they,
and how do you move a stone larger than a miller's
    wheel,
and why do you take a body whose injury is carrion?
The loved unnamed disciple outruns Simon Peter
and stooping down and looking at the void
sees the linens and the napkin
where the crown of thorns had been
just lying there. But he does not go in,
it is Peter who goes in in order to believe,
for as yet the followers know not the Scripture,
that the son of man must rise again from the dead,
though what is again if not for the first time?
Peter and _____ leave Mary at the tomb, weeping,
mourning both the death and disappearance,

then she, too, looks into the darkness
only to see an angel robed in white
sitting at the head of where the body was,
another sitting at the feet. And the angels ask her,
Woman, why weepest thou?
Because, she answers, they have taken away my Lord,
at which moment, turning, she sees someone standing
who repeats the angels' question and asks, Whom
    seekest thou?
Perhaps her tears have blinded her, since she thinks the
    man,
of all things, is the gardener,
and thinks he may have helped remove the body,
as if, in her distraction, a grave is like a garden.
When do we know what we are meant to know?
When we know it? When we know it.
Mary hears the voice of her own name,
and in the same voice Jesus says to her,
Touch me not, for I have not yet ascended,
but go back and speak of this to those to whom it
    matters.
What is the first day of the week, the third day?
It is the day of the body between worlds.
Therefore that evening when Jesus reappears,
wounded with death but once again alive,
he is able to breathe on these disciples the breath
of the Holy Ghost, the breath of belief.
Thomas, called Didymus, one among the twelve,
is not with them and later must be told,

as if it is a story, something wished for.
Thomas the Doubter, Thomas the Pragmatist,
says to the remnant, Except I shall see in his hands
the print of the nails, and thrust my hand
into his side, I will not believe.
And Jesus, eight days after the first,
returns and says to the Doubting Thomas,
Reach hither thy finger and behold my hands;
and reach hither thy hand, and thrust it into my side:
blessed are they that have not seen, and yet have
    believed.
Which is why, surely, he would not let Mary,
though herself reborn, touch him.

Dayton

1

dark wine

It's hard to give up first passages
or those that, the longer they go back,
almost disappear, time in its shadow space,
near shapelessness, and the dead voice now pure.
My grandmother's younger brother had a voice
so weak he seemed always to be speaking
from a corner, in recession to spent passion
or some forgotten anger, who'd lied about his age
to join the war, at fifteen, nineteen sixteen.
Paul, I think, Paul Debrae, favoring those bone
white sleeveless undershirts popular in film-noir
forties movies, the rationing of light a single lamp,
the furniture a chest, a bed, a chair, a pretty picture.
Whole American cities night-lit in wartime dusk.
While Paul's Italian wife, a rose Rose, gave off
a kind of sunlight Sundays with spaghetti
and meatballs big as baseballs. . . . Rose,
never in a corner, their crowded, witching house
fronting on an alley-like side street,
off Siebanthaler or a name more German.
Then the kitchen stove, an icebox, fresh-made bread,

dark and darker wine, a sauce that looked like blood,
the orders of the odors rising and falling.
I don't remember being taller than the table,
which meant my field of vision hit people
at the waist. A belt, a wraparound half apron,
a flowering dress folding at the hips.
Propped on pillows, I ate the long red pasta
the way I'd just been taught: to turn the fork
like a working tool, something to think about,
as if eating were a job or art, until each mouthful
bled inside the mouth—.

2

a rhyme for Harry

Like an orphanage on fire, the purest possible ascension,
like children disappeared into spirit up in smoke,
like the son he's claimed has burned in a house
whose site on Sundays he takes you to as if it were
the grave and you the child of witness, Harry alive,
Harry an orphanage himself, after the war to end all war,
flush with fear of fire or worse over the open air
of the trenches, Harry mincing, Harry sinking in his
        chair
by the full-length Philco, surrounded by the burnholes
of his sick cigar, souring into sleep, his boy-sized feet
still short of the floor, or those hours ago shoveling
bituminous wet coal into furnaces at French Oil,
then walking the two miles home from work looking
        like
he's wearing someone's clothes, the hole in the picture,
the relative you cross the street to miss, the one,
in your mind, you kill. And since he's German, sullen,
Sullenberger, close enough, and since he's the clown
of his own pain, with his pathos and invective
and detective magazines, in which women are abused
in lipstick pinks and reds, and since he stutters
in Dutchman English in front of his hardest feelings,
and likely watched his son, if he ever had one, disappear
in one form or another, he's responsible for the next

world
war or if not fire the air incendiary, Harry pissed,
Harry staggering, with help, to get to bed,
where he lights up in the sober dark to think his
    thoughts
and wonder how he's made it this far, the doughboy
left for dead, the father of a memory, who Sundays holds
your hand and follows the same story to its sad,
frayed conclusion, Harry lying, Harry crying
into his urine-yellow beer, toasting the bitter end
to the burning air—.

3
kittyhawks

Stories of great clouds stacked due north of here.
My mother's mother's father in too-bright ocean
sunlight, trying to teach angle and foil,
lift and flow, the sailshape of a wing.
Not to imagine anything higher yet connected,
nor how the string tightens yet goes slack
at the rise and set, the wind blowing on a line
like a wave. Still alive, still coming down
the stairs learning to walk, bicycle clips
and cap, ready to ride the bike bought
from the Wrights, in Dayton, back in the rain
and mist still forming. Bicycle wheels with wings,
bicycle double gears lifting into the camera,
into the sea air's endlessness, the shutter speed
slowing just enough. To stand on the coast
of this part of Carolina is to join the wind—
in December, the leeward-to-landward shipwreck side.
For a man to fly he moves across and out and never stops.
Only Orville-in-the-air holds on. The granite
Wright Memorial the gravestone where they start,
first with the gliders, then with the power,
and tracks along a line to sail a train.
Someone taking pictures of the two flying kites—
boxy, triangular, sailcloth blown to rags—
that look like, in the blur of the turn
of the century, ours—.

Nature

Once in a while we can afford to lose
a negligible number of a thing
and not know exactly the species, specs,
or certain cold science of what was lost.
The two or more Latinate field sparrows
that flew into my loft, blown by the wind
or made more curious because the porch door
was open, didn't have the least chance
against O.P., my gray *Felis catus domesticus,*
who caught them, I assume, losing flight,
since I came back home to find their wing
and body feathers scattered on the floor
and furniture, signs of the *genera*
of what they had been: Chipping, Brewer's,
Tree, or Black-Chinned Sparrow, the rest
of what they were (fill in the blank) missing.
The Venerable Bede has the sparrow fly
through a door or window of a warm mead hall
in order to escape death in winter,
the irony of which can be lost in his parable
of how a single life compares to the length
of time it will take a bird to navigate
its way back out, say a door or window

on the opposite side, life flying away
from death back into death, ice, fire,
and ice again, a circle more than a cycle.

Nurture

In 627, King Edwin of Northumbria
summons his council to discuss whether
or not this Christ is the Fountain
of Life, the Sun, or simply son of man.

Coifi, one of the king's wise men, has argued that "the
religion which we have hitherto professed has, as far as
I can learn, no virtue in it." Coifi, a man of self-interest,
asserts that "none of your people has applied himself
more diligently to the worship of our gods than I, and
yet there are many who receive greater favors from you
and are more preferred than I and are more prosperous
in all their undertakings. Now if the gods were good for
anything they would forward me, who have been more
careful to serve them. If on examination you find these
new doctrines, which are now preached to us, better and
more effective, we must receive them without delay."

Whereupon, one of the king's chief courtiers adds
that "the present life of man, O king, seems to me, in
comparison to that time which is unknown to us, like
the swift flight of a sparrow through the room wherein
you sit at supper in winter with your commanders
and ministers and a good fire in the midst, while the

storms of rain and snow prevail abroad. The sparrow, I
say, flying in at one door and out at another, while he is
within, is safe from wintry blast, but after a short space
of fair weather he immediately vanishes out of your sight
into the dark winter from which he has emerged. So this
life of man appears for a while, but of what went before
or what will follow we are utterly ignorant. If, therefore,
this new doctrine contains something more certain it
seems justly to deserve to be followed."

Darkness and emptiness, death weather
of the North, Wordsworth, at Windermere,
quoting his own Venerable Bede, how the bird
is that small "transient thing," and "what world"

it comes from, "what woe or weal"
on its departure waits, we'll fail
to know, at least through winter, when
the reborn spring and Skiddaw's brilliant green

arrive. But one "Christmas-time," the boy, his father
barely in the ground, 1783, on a high tor
in the wind, remembers, in the poem, the woman torn,
the animal alone, the ruined tree, the rain

inside its song echoing the "old stone wall"—

                                     "All
these were spectacles and sounds to which / I often
would repair, and thence would drink / As at a fountain."

As Reported

Somewhere in the word *casualty* is the word *casual,*
and what they share is chance, the accident,
the unexpected interval, the arbitrary nature
of the natural: or unnatural, like the woman
in the picture in the news, her face obscured,
her covered head half-bowed as if in prayer,
whose right arm is severed at the shoulder
from a car bomb in a marketplace in the Al Jabbar
suburb of old Baghdad, who becomes the captured
soldier beheaded in the district of Dahana-ye
Ghori in a province in the north, Afghanistan.
And so on, as reported: people once collateral
cut to size or killed, turning little death
to larger death then back again to small,
only, by tomorrow, the paper they were printed on.
Meanwhile, the birds, the blackcaps, the fan-tails,
and fifty names or more of other warblers,
plus owls and hawks and golden orioles,
lamented if not prized for their beauty
or their song, are missed by the thousands,
maybe millions, in Cyprus and in general
the Aegean, where they're caught in traps
of lime-sticks and mist-netting: hard to believe
the animal need for protein from something

hardly hand-sized and literally light as feathers.
Or is it the feather in the voice we're after,
the secret of the *chip,* the *chir,* the *tew,*
or the feather in the cap, the sign of victory?
Birds in the billions, the elegant article says,
"flooding up from Africa . . . avian populations"
becoming, bird by bird, "sub-optimal."

The Day of the Failure in Saigon, Thousands in the Streets, Hundreds Killed, A Lucky Few Hanging On the Runners of Evacuating Copters

Old arguments among old arguments
about the common species, late into the night,
nineteen sixty-eight, give or take a year,
give or take uncivil disobedience,
cities terrorized, the assassin honing in,
and the example still in front of us
the draft and Vietnam, with the evening
TV Cronkite, the generals' guarantees,
the lottery of dead, the Johnson/Nixon
death mask filling up the screen,
villages destroyed like magic with a match,
a naked burning girl no bigger than a stick
running toward the camera, a man, Viet
Cong, looking at the lens, his face already
oatmeal, while here, on the other side
of the pictures, all two hundred of our human
bones intact, the vestiges, appendages
in place, the Jacob's ladder following
the spine, the warm brain within the cold

brain—or reverse, reptilian, mammalian—
traces of the graduating faunae and their gods
lingering inside us yet alien as children,
and there's a bird, a kind of bird,
alive in there, too, between the raptor
and the wren, of a size we can't imagine,
soaring in the thermals or secret in the hedge
speaking in the bird-talk we call singing,
a missing link along the chain of being.

Black Walnuts

I was at that age that if a stone fit the hand you threw it,
the smaller the target the larger the hit, though that was relative
to size and distance, a starling, say, compared to a crow, each
a pestilence, the one up close, ubiquitous, and nervous, the other
noisy, far, and ponderous, and besides, with stones, it was
impossible, so we threw at the possible trees, at the long lower
branches, and after that at the stand-out leaves. We'd been told
that a thing worth doing was worth doing well, if only difficult,
like testing buckeyes on the big horse chestnut, locked in fruit
like fat around a heart, fat enough to be picked apart—in the poem
of eyes you can see me now lifting my right arm, ready to throw at
buck's eyes, named on purpose in a tree named for the horse that
    eats them.

You wear out your arm before you hit even one,
until October or the afternoon is gone.

Or on another day another tree, a walnut, its flowering
feathering of leaves less burdensome, the furrowed trunk itself
darkly tall, darker in the fall, which made it easier to see what
you were aiming at: "the thick semi-fleshy, yellowish-green husks,"
yet "the hanging fruit of Jove," the kind of fact or myth you love
in school—and when the teacher cut a walnut to the quick to show
the cortex of the shell she wanted us to think the human brain

and wonder at its look-alike strange look, but went too far, Miss
Pike, to say that eating one might make a difference to our small
minds and confidence. Besides, we didn't have to hit them after all.
The walnuts fell and fell, and if you picked them up before they
    rotted
they fit the hand like stones, and, better, they were round.

From the Window of the Quiet Car

1

Insular as a Quaker meeting.
How in silence the speed of the several landscapes
    quickens,
how the money green of the intermittent trees
    multiplies.
How the brick industrial ruins take on integrity again,
as if fast light has at last erased the muscle-bound
    graffiti.
How the oil on the native waters mixes and unmixes.
How the basic houses and the backsides of small cities
    blend,
one heavy dog on a leash with its heavy urban owner.
How the white sun dapples, goes away, comes back as
    glare.
How the words of the sometimes book move
    independently.
How the mind is afloat, adrift, finding its way in gravity.
How to sleep, now to sleep, off and on, sitting up like a
    child.
How to hear what someone's inspired to say already too
    out loud
into an ear, a cellphone, or the meditating air.

2

Thee for my recitative—
the long whistle, long shadow, at so many miles an hour,
the wheels, if there are wheels, a trailing echo,
yet inside the inside, stillness, if you close your eyes.
All you had to do was cross the cut cornfield and stand
    there
and train after lonesome train would pass on schedule,
boxcars, flatcars, coal cars open,
the rails taking tickets, taking tickets, taking tickets,
and sometimes, on the faster runs, actual people looking
    out
like strangers to futures at speeds overwhelming,
but waving, nevertheless, at this small boy waving back
like the past receding. These were the fall afternoons
    after
school—at night, watching from a distance, it was little
    lines
of light or nothing but the dark taking tickets.

The Sand

The dream goes that I'm somewhere on a walk
in a city like Seattle, heading down a hill
in a light-to-heavy rain that makes the brick
as slick as glass or what we say when the ground
is moving with us or what we mean when the ground
feels dangerous. I've left a place I know
or thought I knew and could find my way back to,
but by the time I slip-slide to the city's open
depth I'm in among a twist of buildings someone
might remember from a childhood, though he'll
never know for certain how or why he got there,
including a hotel whose silent lobby smells
of camphor and old age with its worn-out mahogany
and checkerboard tile floor and ceiling
stained with smoke from a century of tobacco
and the paper-yellow small talk of secrecy.
Then a single fragile burning chandelier.
The man behind the desk is kind in the manner
of the helpless, so that when I ask directions
he has no idea, as I have no idea, except a fear
of falling or closure. The rain by now is falling
heavily, breaking on the windows, the looming
nothing sky sealed in as if it were a final
structure ready, as in myth, to come down all

at once. I'm almost happy here. The city rain,
the ceiling rain, rain like a sudden jail,
each drop of it as countless as the glassy sand
on beaches, as stars, among the dust, are comparable
in numbers. Sunlight will never show again.
I'll never, where I am, get back to where I started.

Canto XVIII

In Lower Hell there are pockets of a place
    called Maleborge, closing on the Center
    of the Earth, of stone the color of the pig
iron in the high hard walls that guard it,
    at whose core is an abyss
    with ten terraced layers circling to the edge
like ramparts of a castle defended by its moats
    or bridges from ten thresholds arching
    into waves to where the bridging ends.
So we found ourselves abandoned here,
    once Geryon set us down, my guide ahead
    just left of where we walked, while on the right
below, in the first dry ditch, new misery,
    new torments, new naked souls
    mock-marching in a lockstep coming toward us,
others on the other side going in our direction
    as quickly as the Romans the year of Jubilee,
    to keep the crowds in motion, divided
their slow passage on the bridge,
    eyes dead straight, some headed to St. Peter's
    toward the Castle, some headed to the Mount.
And left and right, along the moat-like ditch,
    I saw horned demons practicing their whips,
    lashing the nameless backs of souls,

while any loafers where the stragglers were
    paid for their loafing until they jumped
    just out of reach of the next whip-crack.
One I recognized seemed to know me,
    so I said, as if speaking past him,
    "I think this could be someone I once knew.
May we not linger here to study him?"
    And of course my patient guide allowed me
    to step back as close as possible
to this lost soul, who, hoping to hide himself
    by looking down, became more visible.
    "You who cast your eyes away, whose profile
I recognize, are Venedico Caccianemico.
    Why are you here among this waste and pain?"
    He answered that he would say nothing
if he could, "but who controls memory?
    In your living voice I hear the vital world
    again. I was the one who placed Ghisolabella
under the Marquis's will, whatever else the hearsay
    of the details of the story. I'm not
    the only Bolognese weeping in this hole.
We so fill its space that there are more of us
    than all the tongues capable of *sipa*
    between the Reno and Savena,
as if you didn't know already of our famous avarice."
    And even as he spoke the lash was laid—
    "Pimp move on, you'll find no women to seduce
along this path." With that I turned to find
    my guide, and in a few more well-worn steps

came to a stark rock bridging promontory
that we climbed with ease and followed to its right,
    by way of leaving these now shadows
    of eternal circlings. When we reached
a special passage in the stone cut for more sinners
    under lash, my guide said, "Stay awhile
    to take a look at those coming into view,
whose faces were obscure because they've been
    behind us, whose souls belong to users
    and deceivers." Therefore we looked down
the column driven forward, the mercy of the whip
    no less laid on. "See that great one,"
    my guide volunteered, "who handles pain
without the pain of tears, how he seems the king,
    this Jason, who by courage and device,
    relieved the men of Colchis of the Fleece,
and later, when he happened past the strange isle
    of Lemnos, where the loveless women put their men
    to death, spread honey on his words to gull
the famed beguiler, Hypsipyle, and left her there,
    pregnant, forsaken—this Jason's guilt
    condemns him now, and even more through
    vengeance
of Medea. This slavery with him are deceivers,
    too, swallowed here forever for their sins."
    By now we were coming to the ridge that narrows
the embankment serving as a basis for yet
    another bridge until we heard

the whining and the snorting and the beating
of dead palms against the useless purging
     of dead flesh. Like steam or vapor
     from a privy pit their sullied exhalations
rose in humid air so thick they stuck and crusted
     over, sick to the eye and nose, their privy
     depths deep beyond our sight, until we got
to the crown of the arch overhang that permitted
     us to see these human forms mired
     in a flood of excrement, as in an overflow
of sewers. My eyes, compelled to see more than
     I wanted, saw one bare head so covered
     up in waste you couldn't tell lay from clergy.
The head spoke out. "Why do you stare at me
     more than at these others just as foul?"
     "Because," I said, "if I remember well,
I know you from when your hair was dry—
     you're Alessio Interminel of Lucca
     even in your new-found disguise."
And as if his head were something not quite his,
     he beat it with both hands. "Down here
     my flatteries become just what they are."
At which moment my guide and leader said,
     "Lean forward now a little past these souls
     to see the one who scratches to the blood
with her filthy, excremental nails
     and fidgets up and down, squatting
     then standing—it's Thais the whore, who

once answered her lover's question about the value
of the pleasure he bestowed by saying
it was value almost beyond the cost."

after Dante

Imaginary Prisons

A Piranesian interior. Operatic space.
Bridges, balconies, arches, trusses, piers,
pendulous chains dropped straight or tied
like bellropes, incense burners hooked to the ends
like jewels. The texture a charcoal smoke of paper
worked, reworked, then left for a while,
some of the structures paler, for perspective,
most of them as massive as invented Roman ruins,
stairs and broken stairwells leading away
like passages within the various body.
Fear of the dark, fear of locked doors,
visible lines drawn to vanishing points.
A city built sub rosa, like Venice,
celestially domed over, with soft night
leaking in, water reflecting water,
via vulva, vagina, vestibule.

Human Excrement

The detail and the distinguishing odor,
the sight of it in nature,
the sight of it at all,
the odd fragment on the sidewalk
or along the edge of the skeletal shrub,
where those who constantly look down
or feel small in the world
see the new order as a trail of pins,
mother-of-pearl, or parts
of the iridescence of a starling.

Whoever it was had to squat down hard,
then harder in the dark
near the trees off Q
and hold breath like a diver,
had to shut out headlights streaming 23rd
and someone walking past too close,
as the failed intimacy of the body
was once more added and subtracted,
this answer to longing
and what is finally left of us.

Caravaggio's *Conversion*

Paul, in Corinth, separating flesh from flesh,
one kind of men—by which he means of women—
one kind of beasts, another of the fishes,
and another of the birds. And bodies celestial
as well as terrestrial, different glories,
the glory of the sun and the glory of the moon,
each visible star a glory, each invisible star
about to be. Then he asks, beyond the body,
how the body can be raised, yours and mine,
except the other flesh—animal, grain, and stone—
be changed. He means, he says, the spiritual body,
as different from the natural as earth from air,
as air is different from yet part of gravity.
As if, say, we'd fallen from a horse on a road
somewhere between here and Damascus because
a kind of light out of nowhere was blinding
and the height of the fall was the weight
of our whole life up till now—how to be lifted,
how to be made to see again but different—

At Seventy-one

How simple a thing seems when you think back to its
    source,
like a river that starts out smaller than a stream
north of Duluth and ends in the Gulf as the body
of "a strong brown god," the means to the end
finally one in the same, as memory and the moment
are one in the same—this dawn, for instance,
October on the calendar but heat still piled
from the filled sky down, wet enough to rain,
though it won't, it'll just hang fire,
the way a wound of sunrise in an hour
in northern Minnesota will be blood-in-the-eye
before it clears above the harvest or what is left
of the harvest to be plowed under in order to wait
for the first frost then the first snow that is already
likely high in the air like the dust off fields far upriver
where the waters begin, turn south, and become the
    Mississippi.

Orphan Hours

When. When, the beginning of a temporal adverbial subordination, pending or depending, but always to wend one's way, and not to be confused with the wen on the left side of my great-grandfather Lyn's forehead, the size of a small doorknob and no less crystalline a cyst than all that was otherwise sebaceous in his system and the source of his ninety-seven-year-old wisdom, since to touch it was to move back and forth in time.

In a lifetime you can touch the flesh of the past in sequence with the old, since the old only die to become the next in line, like King Lyn, my father's mother's father, older than the Civil War, whose bloodline in real blood brought me back to life, within the hour, from a blue-baby birth.

Or my mother's mother's father, even older, riding down a hill with me strapped on his back, as if the bike had wings, then standing, holding me, in front of history, to have our picture taken.

My father and my uncles back from war, at a table under a late autumn tree, on a Sunday, playing worn-out ace-a-penny cards with both these brilliant souls whose bodies are the leaves.

The first President I voted for was Kennedy, in
Middletown, where he'd ridden up from Cincinnati
with the top down and the roads lined with children. I
was twenty-turning-twenty-one, working for the year
for paraplegic Louis McCallay, in his Booth Tarkington
mansion, with servants and Eleanor O'Fallon, who was
fading and whose place, as caretaker, I was taking, though
I was months perfecting what it took to keep him just
alive, from catheter to conversation, who'd started his
life of specialists at nineteen, and from there, in his great
wheelchair, had started his life of travel—to Paris, for
example, in the thirties—Henry Miller, Anaïs Nin—
between wars and finally home again and Proust, in French,
in latitudinal long sentences and even longer sentences, flat
as paper, in bed.

I'd lift him as if he were a child, bathe him, and minister
as if he were war-wounded. He was tall and pale and broken
at the glass base of his spine. He lived, like Proust, mostly in
his head, the least detail a winding path, memory in a word.
I'd read him Whitman, as an antidote.

With half your body dead you age twice as fast, thus
Louis was over a hundred. So I give you my sprig of lilac.

Everyone I knew from then is gone, gone years ago, the
line extending miles. My father died on his knees, half a
man, my mother a machine until I had to choose to turn
it off.

Louis, it seemed to me, never rested but instead talked himself, read himself, in paragraphs, to sleep, lying there, always, in one position, in the attitude I saw him at the end. Proust, in Paris, walking the Marais or, later, lying in his cork-lined silent space, testing his memory of a madeleine dipped in a well of lime-blossom tea. . . . These were the hours Louis would wake with, from sessions of sweet silent thought, to be remembered, as if first thing, each morning.

Dusk Coming On Outside
_____, New York

A kind of mountain pond or lake,
the kind of algae-stillness sudden wind kicks up,
the way the spring wind out of Canada is scooping up
    the surface,
forcing the swans to ride in harness,
all pointed in the same direction,
dozens of them, lucent, whiter in the rain,
some of them feeding, some at attention—

a kind of gravity of water gathering the line of where the
    sun
would be, the ghost-dance of the sun,
the pale green clouds of the hillsides lifting,
blurring on the windshield's mica-points of light,
miles of the storm's bright scalloping
bending into wavelengths through the glass
with the fluency of water, water's cold gray eyes.

The Lost Wine

Not so lost as it is the last of the wine
in the bowl of the glass I've emptied
as an offering to the blue tumble of the sea
off the high coast outside one of those cliff

Italian towns between the Lombardy walls
of pines and the oblivion. And why this
happy gesture except to please some excess
in the heart, except the wine was heart's blood

entering and leaving. I like to think
it gives some something back to what the sea
has lost, something more than the simple rain
falling through its miles to bless the water.

Look down with me right now at the long face
of the deep—the waves are drunk, their color changed!

after Valéry

On the Beach at Duck

The almost gray brown pelicans flying in from nowhere
and as far as the eye can see flying out to nowhere,
though they do it to perfection in formation
above the invisible lines drawn perfectly in sand
and the inching blowback waves measuring the shore,
since once inside the wind they hardly move their wings,
except to readjust or sometimes change the leader,
until once inside the light they're gone.

On the Lawn at the Forians

Terrible the wind topping out the trees.
The immensely visible wind filling
the blue trees bluer with the blue dusk.
The infinitesimal evening settling.

Stay awhile, you want to say to the sun.
Because summer is terrible and meant
to hold on till the last possible moment.
Like tonight, once more, the long day ending.

And just as the trees release what is left
of the light, just as the wind releases
its weight, the sky, the forgiving sky, lifts
it all, gathers it all into place.

Terrible this blue that is now the sky.
Blue as the breath rising darkly into air.
Someone saying something too quiet to hear.
But the birds are listening, almost silently.

And you want to say to the sun, again,
stay, even as it's suddenly passing.
Terrible this blue radiant dark rising.
Terrible the wind and the light nothing.

Leavings

To walk out of this flesh, leave the body of the bones.
To undress utterly, so that even love and mirrors
and the voice inside your head wouldn't know you.
To write your name in cold blood by a candle
whose flame would fire air, breath, everything,
including paper. To be totally absent from yourself,
from thought of yourself, to forget yourself entirely.
To go out only at night, naked to the soles,
perpetually catching cold, and in fear of footprints
walk on your hands. They'd think *five-toed bird,*
and at the edge of water imagine flight.
But you'd still be walking, if you could,
out of body, out of time, leaving behind, in a wake
of absence, clothes, fingerprints, ashes, words—

DEDICATIONS

"Lapsed Meadows"/James Wright 1927–1980

"The Jay"/Margaret Rose Plumly

"Lost Key"/Esther Plumly 1918–1994

"Four Hundred Mourners"/Rosemary and Andrew Forian

"Look for Me"/Howard Norman and David Wyatt

"Vesper Sparrow"
"Afterward"
"Wistman's Wood"
"On Dartmoor"/Deborah Digges 1950–2009

"Arbitrarily"/Richard Hugo 1923–1982

"Blind"/John Auchard

"Amidon Christmas Tree Farm Cardinal"/
Kathleen and Wayne Amidon

"Sitting Alone in the Middle of the Night"/
Herman Plumly 1916–1972

"On the Lawn at the Forians"/Dawn and Stephen Forian